little monsters

cookbook

recipes and photographs by
zac williams

GIBBS SMITH
TO ENRICH AND INSPIRE HUMANKIND

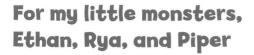

**For my little monsters,
Ethan, Rya, and Piper**

First Edition
14 13 12 11 10   8 7 6 5 4

Text and Photographs © 2010 Zac Williams

Published by
Gibbs Smith
P.O. Box 667
Layton, Utah 84041

1.800.835.4993 orders
www.gibbs-smith.com

www.monsterscook.com

Cover designed by Sheryl Dickert Smith
Manufacture in Shenzhen, China, in August 2010 by Toppan Printing Co..
Gibbs Smith books are printed on either recycled, 100% post-consumer
waste, FSC-certified papers, or on paper produced from a 100%
certified sustainable forest/controlled wood source.

Library of Congress Cataloging-in-Publication Data

Williams, Zac.
  Little monsters cookbook : recipes and photographs / by Zac Williams.
— 1st ed.
     p. cm.
  ISBN-13: 978-1-4236-0600-0
  ISBN-10: 1-4236-0600-0
  1. Cookery—Juvenile literature. 2. Monsters in art—Juvenile literature.
I. Title.
  TX652.5.W5524 2010
  641.5—dc22
                              2010001323

Contents

The Deliciously Gruesome Guide to Monster Meals

Life as a monster is hard enough without worrying about what's for dinner. Fortunately in this book, you will find all the recipes you need to prepare a ghastly feast for you and your creepy crew. Even those creatures of the night with particularly picky palates will find something tempting enough to sink their teeth into.

Just remember as you plan your monster menu to make sure you add foods that are tasty and good for you too. Even Frankenstein knows that eating right is a big part of staying fit and one step ahead of the pitchfork-carrying villagers! So try to eat all kinds of healthy foods and save the sweets for dessert.

Most importantly, remember that the more fun you have cooking, the better the food will taste! So cook monster-style and mix it up by asking your family and friends to help with the preparation. And don't forget to serve your food with your best monster manners. Set the table in a spooky style and you are sure to freak out your guests. So get those fangs, claws, and feet ready to become a ghoulish gourmet of fine creature cuisine. Let's dig in . . . at least six feet under!

Staying Safe

Your blood is a very precious thing. Just ask Dracula. To preserve all of that great red stuff it is important to follow safety rules while in the kitchen. Here are important tips to keep you from getting hurt.

- Always ask an adult to help when using the stove, microwave, or oven. Never use a cooking range or microwave without supervision to help you avoid burns and fires.

- Knives can be very dangerous. Have a grown-up help you chop or cut any ingredients that require a sharp blade. Don't ever play with kitchen knives. They are tools for use in cooking only.

- Small kitchen appliances such as blenders and food processors help make cooking easier, but they should always be used with an adult's assistance. Never put utensils or hands into these appliances.

- Wash your hands with soap and warm water before beginning to cook and wash your hands often while cooking to keep germs out of what you are making.

- Make sure to properly refrigerate foods that can easily spoil such as meats, dairy products, eggs, and other foods that need refrigeration. This helps you avoid sickness from bacteria in the food.

- Never use the same plate that raw food has been on for serving food.

- Keep your kitchen work area clean and organized. Clean up spills quickly so you or someone else doesn't slip. Keep towels and other items that could catch on fire away from the stove.

- Sometimes you might need a boost to reach the kitchen counter, but be very careful to only stand on a safe stepping stool so you don't fall.

- And most importantly always ask for permission and help from a grown-up when you want to cook so they can make sure that you have fun in the kitchen!

Mix It, Cook It, Chomp It

Before you begin as a monster in the kitchen it helps to know a few things about how to cook. With a little practice, you soon will be at the head of your creepy class as an expert in the delicious dark arts! Here are some tips you should know.

Measuring Dry Ingredients: When you measure dry ingredients such as flour and sugar you will use measuring cups, usually 1 cup, 1/2 cup, 1/3 cup, and 1/4 cup. Fill the correct measuring cup to the top, but not over, with your ingredient. Sometimes it helps to use a butter knife to level off the extra. Remember to keep track of how many cups you add by counting.

Measuring Liquid Ingredients: You can use the same measuring cups that you use for dry ingredients when you measure liquids like milk or oil, but it is easier to use a clear glass measuring cup. That way you can see the liquid inside and read how much you've added to the cup by using the marks on the outside.

Measuring with Spoons: Sometimes you will need to measure ingredients in teaspoons and the bigger tablespoons. It is best to use cooking measuring spoons that are exactly the right size. Just add the ingredient and scrape off the extra with a butter knife until the ingredient is level with the top of the spoon.

Adding Ingredients: Have all of your ingredients out and ready to go before starting a recipe. Then add the ingredients following the order the recipe tells you.

Keeping Clean: The cleaner you keep the kitchen while you cook the easier it is to clean up when you are done. Try to put dirty dishes and utensils in the sink as soon as you are done with them. An apron can help you keep yourself clean. Remember to wash your hands often with soap and warm water.

Experiment and Have Fun: Cooking is about being creative. Maybe you'll have a great idea for something different in a recipe. You can even try mixing together your favorite flavors into a totally new combination. Have fun and keep cooking!

Wolfsbane Elixir

While many werewolves are content to live the life of a monster, other more progressive types claim this elixir lets them retain their human shape. But don't take my word for it.

Makes 2 drinks

Blue decorating sugar

Crushed ice

$1/2$ cup blue raspberry–
   flavored Italian syrup*

I liter sparkling water

$1/4$ cup half-and-half

1 Prepare two glasses by wetting rims and dipping them into the blue decorating sugar. Fill each glass three-fourths of the way full with crushed ice.

2 Add $1/4$ cup blue raspberry syrup to each glass. Then fill each glass almost to the top with sparkling water.

3 Add a splash of half-and-half to each glass and enjoy!

*You can substitute any other colorful flavor if you like.

Full-Moon Howlers

When you're out running with the pack under a full moon, these delicious two-bite sandwiches are just what a canine craves to quiet a growling stomach.

Makes 12 mini sandwiches

24 precooked frozen meatballs

1 cup ketchup

1/4 cup brown sugar

1 teaspoon mustard

12 small buns or dinner rolls

Lettuce

Tiny dill pickles

1 Heat the frozen meatballs in the microwave or oven following the package directions. Make sure the meatballs are completely heated throughout.

2 Add ketchup, brown sugar, and mustard to a large saucepan over medium heat. Cook and stir until the sauce just begins to boil. Remove from heat. Add the heated meatballs and stir to coat the meatballs with the sauce.

3 Place 2 meatballs on each bun or roll. Add a leaf of lettuce and a pickle on top. Serve immediately.

Werewolf Skins

Werewolf skin is tough enough to withstand just about anything except for a silver bullet, but cooked just right it sure is tasty. Enjoy these cheesy snacks with a bit of bite.

Makes 6 werewolf skins

3 large baked potatoes

3 tablespoons butter
   or margarine, melted
   and divided

3/4 teaspoon all seasoned salt

3 strips bacon, cooked
   and crumbled

3/4 cup sour cream, divided

1/2 cup grated
   cheddar cheese

2 tablespoons
   chopped chives

1 Preheat oven to 475°F. Lightly spray a baking sheet with nonstick cooking spray.

2 Cut the baked potatoes in half lengthwise. Scoop out the potato inside to within about 1/2 inch of the skins. In a bowl, mix the scooped out potato, 2 tablespoons of the melted butter, all seasoned salt, crumbled bacon, and 1/2 cup of the sour cream.

3 Brush the outside of the potato skins with the remaining tablespoon of butter. Spoon the potato and sour cream mixture equally into the skins. Top each with some of the grated cheddar cheese.

4 Bake the skins for 8 to 10 minutes or until the cheese is melted. Serve immediately topped with the remaining sour cream and chives.

Claws of the Yeti

Few people know that the yeti is a Far Eastern cousin of the werewolf. Beware the yeti's claws, unless of course they happen to be these tasty Asian appetizers.

Makes 24 bundles

24 round pot sticker wrappers

1 (8-ounce) package cream cheese, softened

2 green onions, finely chopped

1/2 cup prepared sweet-and-sour sauce plus more for serving

4 to 6 tablespoons canola or vegetable oil

1 Open the pot sticker wrappers. In the center of a wrapper, place a spoonful of cream cheese, a few chopped green onions, and a small drizzle of sweet-and-sour sauce. Moisten edges with water, fold in half, and seal. Repeat for remaining pot stickers.

2 Heat the oil in a skillet over medium-high heat. Add the prepared bundles, two or three at a time, cooking on each side about 2 minutes until puffy, golden, and crispy. Transfer to a plate lined with paper towels and let drain.

3 Serve immediately with more sweet-and-sour sauce for dipping.

Wolf-Bitten Cupcakes

The secret to becoming a werewolf is to be bitten by a werewolf. While most people find that they are quite happy to remain human, these cupcakes are perfect for those that thirst for a life on the wild and hairy side.

Makes 18 to 24 cupcakes

1 box devil's food cake mix

1 (8-ounce) jar seedless raspberry jam

1 can prepared cream cheese frosting

2 to 3 cups shredded coconut

Various decorator frostings and gels

1 Prepare cupcakes following the instructions on box. Bake and allow to cool.

2 Preheat oven to 400°F. Place coconut in a shallow baking dish and toast for about 5 to 7 minutes. You will need to have your adult supervisor help you stir the coconut a few times during the baking process until it is brown.

3 Microwave the raspberry jam in a glass bowl on high for 30 seconds. Stir until smooth. Set aside 2 tablespoons of jam in a separate bowl.

4 Using a small paring knife, cut a circular wedge out of the top of each cupcake. Spoon some raspberry jam in each and replace the top part of the cupcakes.

5 Frost the cupcakes with the cream cheese frosting. Top with toasted coconut. Use decorator frosting and gels to create ears, eyes, nose, mouth, and fangs. Add reserved raspberry jam on the tips of the werewolves' fangs.

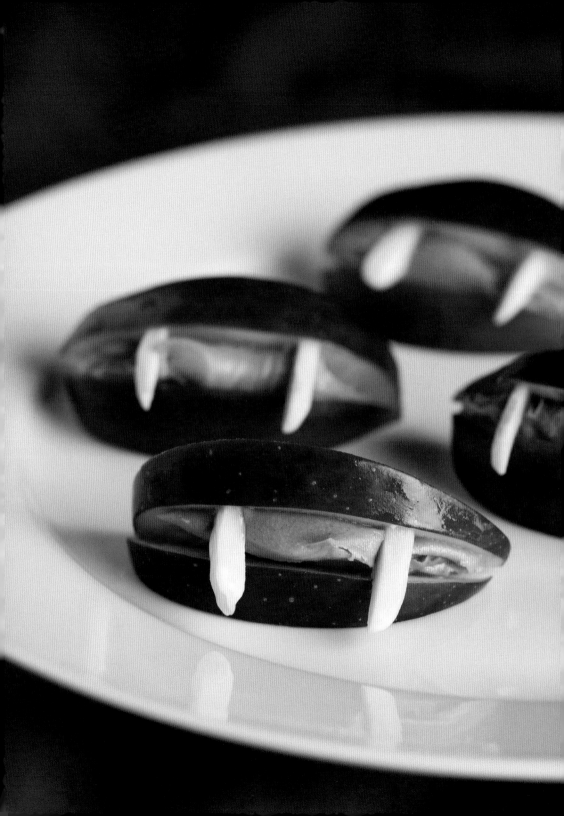

Vampire Bites

When the sun goes down, our friendly bloodsuckers are ready for the night shift. These little bites hit the spot when liquid nourishment is hard to find.

Makes 8 bites

2 medium Red
   Delicious apples
1/2 cup creamy peanut butter
1/2 cup slivered almonds,
   blanched
Chocolate syrup (optional)

1 Core the apples, but don't peel them. Slice each apple into 8 wedges.

2 Spread peanut butter onto half of the apple wedges. Press slivered almonds into one side of each apple wedge to create scraggily teeth.

3 Place an apple slice with the peanut butter side up and top with another apple slice without peanut butter to form a mouth with red lips and teeth.

4 Drizzle with chocolate syrup if desired.

Coffin Crunchers

Sometimes when you are up all night causing monster mischief you just need something to tide you over till morning. This snack has a crunch that can be heard through six feet of soil.

Makes 6 servings

6 round pitas (not
   pocket pita)

3 tablespoons olive oil

1 teaspoon Italian seasoning

1 cup fresh grated
   Parmesan cheese

2 cups prepared hummus
   or marinara sauce

1 Preheat oven to 425°F. Line two baking sheets with foil.

2 Using a knife or kitchen scissors, cut various size coffin shapes from the pita flatbread. Discard leftover bread. Place the coffin shapes on the baking sheets.

3 Lightly brush each coffin shape with olive oil. Sprinkle with Italian seasoning. Then sprinkle with Parmesan cheese and bake for 10 to 12 minutes until cheese melts. Remove from oven and let cool until crunchy.

4 Serve coffin crunchers with hummus or marinara sauce for dipping.

Prince-of-the-Night Pizza

When a colony of vampire bats flutters by, it's nice to offer them something to eat other than yourself. Invite your undead friends over to enjoy making these tempting vampire-sized pizzas.

Makes 8 individual pizzas

Beast bites (pepperoni)

Smoked werewolf (ham or Canadian bacon slices)

Toadstool morsels (sliced button mushrooms)

Tarantula eggs (black olives)

Paleapple (pineapple chunks)

Igor's delight (sliced green bell peppers)

Frog eyeballs (green olives)

Blood berries (sliced cherry tomatoes)

8 round pitas (not pocket pita)

1 (12-ounce) jar pizza sauce

2 cups shredded mozzarella cheese

Essence of immortality (Italian seasoning)

1 Place each pizza topping in its own bowl or jar on a table or counter. A label identifying each dreadful ingredient is always fun.

2 Spread foil on the bottom oven rack. Preheat oven to 450°F.

3 Place each pita on a plate and spread with 2 tablespoons of pizza sauce. Sprinkle with ¼ cup cheese.

4 Allow guests to decorate their pizzas with whichever ingredients they choose. Sprinkle with Italian seasoning.

5 Place pizzas in the oven directly on the top oven rack. Bake for 5 to 6 minutes until bubbly and crisp.

6 Serve with Garlicky Toast Stakes (page 22).

Garlicky Toast Stakes

What do vampires hate more than garlic? Wooden stakes of course! Here's a tasty recipe that you'll want to serve your vampire friends that you really don't like.

Makes 18 toast stakes

6 slices thick-sliced bread
   or Texas toast

6 tablespoons butter or
   margarine, softened

1/2 teaspoon garlic powder

1 cup shredded
   mozzarella cheese

2 tablespoons
   chopped parsley

1 Preheat oven to 350°F. Lightly spray a baking sheet with nonstick cooking spray.

2 Place the softened butter in a small mixing bowl. Add the garlic powder and mix well. Spread the mixture evenly on the six slices of bread.

3 Trim the crusts off the bread and discard. Cut each slice of bread in thirds. Trim one end of each rectangle of bread into a triangle stake shape. Place the bread stakes on the baking sheet.

4 Evenly sprinkle with cheese and parsley.

5 Bake for 7 to 9 minutes until the toast is brown and the cheese is melted. Serve warm.

Bloody Sundae

The secret ingredient of this sundae is not what you might think!

Makes 6 sundaes

6 chocolate-covered grasshopper cookies

$^{1}/_{2}$ cup prepared vanilla frosting

Red food coloring

1 quart vanilla ice cream

Strawberry syrup

Canned whipped cream

Sprinkles

1 Using a pointed cookie cutter such as a star shape, cut two fang marks each out of 6 chocolate cookies. Set aside cookies to use as a garnish. Save the cutout parts and any extra crumbled cookie.

2 Microwave the vanilla frosting on high for 30 seconds. Stir in several drops of red food coloring. Drizzle the chocolate cookies with the frosting. Place on wax paper in the fridge to set.

3 Drizzle strawberry syrup on the insides and bottom of a clear ice cream dish. Add 2 scoops of vanilla ice cream. Drizzle with more strawberry syrup and top with the cookie crumbles. Garnish with a shot of whipped cream, sprinkles, and a "bitten" chocolate cookie. Repeat for remaining 5 sundaes. Serve immediately.

Count Orlock Chocolate Shake

Dracula loves chocolate, but he likes something else even more. I bet you can guess what that is! This delicious shake is certainly chocolaty, but what exactly are those red chunks?

Makes 2 shakes

4 scoops vanilla ice cream

¾ cup skim milk

4 tablespoons chocolate
   syrup plus more
   for serving

6 maraschino cherries

Canned whipped cream

Grenadine syrup (optional)

1 Place the ice cream, milk, 4 tablespoons chocolate syrup, and 4 cherries in a blender. Blend on high speed until cherries are chopped and the shake is smooth.

2 Pour the shake into 2 glasses. Garnish with whipped cream, a small drizzle of chocolate syrup, and grenadine if you wish.

3 Add a cherry on top of each and serve. Be sure the "fang marks" on the cherry are right side up.

Mummy Pups

Ancient Egypt has its own brand of monster, the mummy. Fortunately these little guys can be taken care of in one quick bite.

Makes 18 to 20 pups

1 (16-ounce) package cocktail wieners or mini hot dogs

1 (8-ounce) can refrigerated breadstick dough

Mustard

Ketchup

1 Preheat oven to 400°F. Lightly spray a baking sheet with nonstick cooking spray.

2 Open the refrigerated dough and roll it out on a smooth surface. Cut each breadstick into thirds. Wrap each mini dog several times with a strip of dough to make mummy bandages.

3 Place mummy pups on the baking sheet and bake for 8 to 10 minutes until golden.

4 Cool slightly and then add two drops of mustard to each for the eyes. Serve with more mustard and ketchup for dipping.

Wrap like a Mummy

This recipe is great for special occasions like Mummy's Day. Be sure to eat it while it's hot—unlike the real thing, you won't want to leave it sitting around for thousands of years!

1 package puff pastry sheets

1 cup chopped cooked
   chicken breast

1 cup sliced button
   mushrooms

$1/2$ cup frozen green peas

$1/4$ cup prepared
   Alfredo sauce

1 cup fresh grated
   Parmesan cheese

1 orange or yellow
   bell pepper

1 Preheat oven to 375°F. Place one sheet of puff pastry dough on the counter for 45 minutes until thawed.

2 Unfold the pastry sheet to form a flattened rectangle of dough. Using a knife or kitchen shears, start on the left edge of dough and cut $1/2$-inch-wide strips one third of the way in toward the center. Repeat on the right edge of the dough, cutting $1/2$-inch-wide strips one third of the way toward the center.

3 On the uncut center of the pastry, spread the chopped chicken, mushrooms, and peas. Pour the Alfredo sauce evenly across the ingredients. Set aside 2 tablespoons of Parmesan cheese and sprinkle the remaining cheese over the chicken mixture.

4 Beginning at the bottom, fold over the strips of pastry to the center, alternating sides. This will create a bandaged look. Shape the filled dough with your hands to look like a mummy's body.

5 Place on a baking sheet that has been lightly sprayed with nonstick cooking spray. Sprinkle the remaining Parmesan cheese over the mummy. Bake for 16 to 18 minutes or until brown and puffy.

6 Decorate with bell pepper slices and pieces cut out in shapes for the eyes and mouth. Serve immediately.

Screams-after-Dark Snack Mix

What do you get when you take a little bite of this and a little bite of that? Screams after dark of course. This sweet-and-salty snack mix is perfect to eat while watching your favorite mummy movie.

Makes 8 servings

3 cups Rice Chex cereal

3 cups Corn Chex cereal

¾ cup roasted salted almonds

¼ cup butter or margarine

¼ cup brown sugar

2 tablespoons honey

1 cup mini pretzel twists

½ cup yogurt-covered raisins

1 cup red licorice bites

1 Preheat oven to 400°F. Line a baking sheet with foil and lightly spray with nonstick cooking spray. Set aside.

2 Combine the cereal and almonds in a large bowl. Set aside.

3 Place butter, brown sugar, and honey in a microwave-safe bowl. Microwave on high, covered loosely, for about 2 minutes, stirring halfway through. Carefully pour the mixture over the cereal and nuts. Stir to coat.

4 Spread the cereal mixture on the prepared baking sheet and bake for 8 minutes. Remove and let cool.

5 Put the pretzel twists, yogurt-covered raisins, and licorice bites in a large serving bowl. Stir in the cooled cereal.

Dusty Old Bones

Be careful if you ever open a monster's closet. You may find a pile of old gnawed-on bones. If properly prepared these dusty bones can be delicious.

Makes 24 cookies

Cookies

2 cups sugar

2 eggs

1 cup shortening, melted

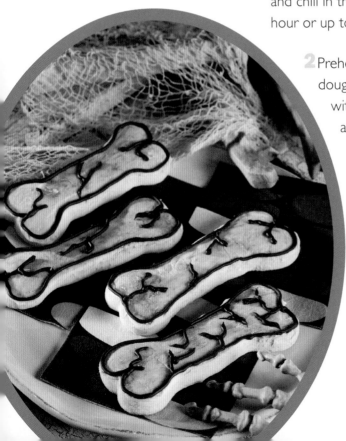

1 In a large bowl, mix together the sugar, eggs, and shortening until smooth and blended. Add the condensed milk, baking powder, salt, and lemon extract stirring well. Mix in the flour, one cup at a time, until the dough is stiff and can be shaped. Cover dough and chill in the refrigerator for at least one hour or up to one day.

2 Preheat oven to 400°F. Roll out the dough on a smooth surface dusted with powdered sugar until it is about ½ inch thick. Using a bone-shaped cookie cutter, cut out cookies and place them on an ungreased cookie sheet.

3 Bake cookies for 7 to 9 minutes until puffy and ever so slightly brown on the edges. Remove from oven and cool on a wire rack.

1 cup evaporated milk

2 teaspoons baking powder

1 teaspoon salt

1 teaspoon lemon extract

5 $\frac{1}{2}$ cups flour

Bone-shaped cookie cutter

Frosting

$\frac{1}{4}$ cup butter or
    margarine, softened

$\frac{1}{4}$ teaspoon salt

$\frac{1}{2}$ teaspoon vanilla extract

3 to 4 cups powdered sugar

Milk

$\frac{1}{4}$ cup cocoa powder

$\frac{1}{4}$ cup powdered sugar

Decorating gel or
    frosting (black, purple,
    or chocolate)

4 Combine the butter, salt, and vanilla in a medium bowl. Add powdered sugar, one cup at a time, beating until frosting is the desired consistency. Add a few drops of milk if the frosting is too thick.

5 In a small bowl, combine cocoa powder with $\frac{1}{4}$ cup powdered sugar. Frost each bone with frosting and dust with the cocoa mixture for an old decayed look. Outline and draw cracks on the bones with the decorating gel. Serve in a big heap.

Trifle with Death

Here's a new twist on a traditional favorite. Best enjoyed in a dank crypt while plundering treasure.

Makes 8 to 10 servings

1 (11-ounce) prepared angel food or sponge cake

1 large box lime gelatin

1 cup mini marshmallows

1 small box instant vanilla pudding

Gummy worms, spiders, frogs, and other gummy candies

2 cups crushed Oreo cookies

1 Tear the cake into pieces about 1 inch in size. Place the cake pieces in the bottom of a glass trifle bowl or other large clear serving bowl.

2 Following the package directions, prepare the gelatin. Pour into the trifle bowl over the cake pieces. Sprinkle the marshmallows over the top.

3 Following the package directions, prepare the pudding. Pour the pudding over the gelatin and cake in the serving bowl. Chill in the refrigerator for at least 2 hours or until the gelatin is set.

4 Using the gummy creatures and the cookie crumbs, decorate the top of the trifle. Spread the Oreo crumbs for dirt and make it look really spooky with worms and creepy candy coming out of the ground!

Frankenstein Zaps

If a spark of lightning can bring Frankenstein's monster to life, just imagine what a zap can do to this delicious snack. Perfect for watching the Monsters vs. Monsters bowl game.

Makes 4 snacks

2 ripe avocados

¼ cup sour cream

1 teaspoon lemon juice

2 tablespoons prepared mild salsa

1 bag guacamole-flavored tortilla chips*

2 cups Mexican blend grated cheese

1 small tomato, diced

1 Peel and pit the avocados. Chop and then mash them in a small bowl. Mix in sour cream, lemon juice, and salsa. Refrigerate for 30 minutes.

2 Arrange tortilla chips on 4 small plates. Sprinkle each with grated cheese.

3 Microwave plates one at a time on high for 30 seconds or until cheese is melted and bubbly. Garnish with Frankie's green dip and diced tomato. Serve immediately.

* Other colored tortilla chips may be substituted.

Frankenfeet

If you notice size 16 boot prints in your garden, you may want to whip up a batch of these sandwiches in case an unexpected, extra-large guest drops by for lunch.

Makes 6 sandwich feet

Foot-shaped cookie cutter
6 slices thick, hearty bread
6 slices ham
6 slices Swiss cheese
1 tablespoon mustard
2 tablespoons mayonnaise
1 can black olives
Leaf lettuce (optional)

1 Using a foot-shaped cookie cutter, cut out a shape from each slice of bread.

2 With the same cookie cutter, cut out a foot-shaped piece of ham and a foot-shaped piece of cheese from each slice.

3 In a small bowl, stir together the mustard and mayonnaise until well blended. Spread the mixture on each foot-shaped piece of bread. Top each with a ham and then a cheese slice. Place on a baking sheet and broil on high for 6 to 8 minutes or until the cheese melts.

4 Decorate with sliced olives to make toes on the feet. A little dab of mustard can be used if needed to set the olives. Serve immediately on a bed of lettuce if desired.

Spare-Parts Salad

This tasty salad is great for when you need to use up leftovers . . . leftover monster parts that is! Don't you just love a plate of nice, juicy eyeballs?

Makes 6 to 8 servings

1 pound green
   seedless grapes

1 pound red seedless grapes

1 cup sour cream

1 (8-ounce) package cream
   cheese, softened

1/2 cup brown sugar

1/2 teaspoon vanilla extract

1 to 2 drops green
   food coloring

Grenadine syrup

Bamboo skewers

1 Wash and remove the grapes from the stems and set aside.

2 In a large serving bowl, mix the sour cream, cream cheese, brown sugar, and vanilla together. Stir in 1 to 2 drops of green food coloring.

3 Fold the grapes into this mixture. Chill, covered, in the refrigerator for at least 2 hours before serving.

4 Spoon into bowls and drizzle with grenadine syrup. Serve with bamboo skewers for stabbing the eyeballs.

Mad Scientist Mix-Up

The evil geniuses that bring us all of those great half-human, half-insect monsters deserve a refreshing break once in a while. Just make sure you drink from the right beaker!

Makes 4 drinks

Ice cubes

1 liter lemon-lime soda

Various food coloring

4 packages Pop Rocks candy

1 Put ice cubes in a beaker-style glass. Pour in lemon-lime soda until it is about an inch from the rim. Add a drop of your favorite mad scientist food coloring and stir gently. Repeat for remaining drinks.

2 Right before drinking your creation dump in a package of Pop Rocks candy and enjoy the crazy reaction!

Important Note: Dry ice can be used to make fun fog effects but *never* put dry ice into anything that will be eaten or drunk. Dry ice can be very dangerous. Children should not handle dry ice—adults only! Ask your adult helper if you want to have dry ice effects for your party.

Creature Cupcakes

Frankenstein enjoyed these delicious self-portrait treats on his first birthday. At age one, he already weighed 285 pounds, was 7 feet tall, and ate 25 cupcakes.

Makes 18 cupcakes

1 chocolate cake mix

1 bag large marshmallows

1 (16-ounce) package
   white candy coating
   or almond bark

Green food coloring

1/2 teaspoon almond extract

1 can purchased
   chocolate frosting

Assorted decorating
   frosting and gels

Green Mike and Ike candies

Assorted candies
   and sprinkles

1 Prepare the cake mix as directed on package. Line a cupcake pan with cupcake wrappers and fill each two-thirds of the way full. Bake according to instructions. Allow cupcakes to cool.

2 Following the package instructions, melt the candy coating in the microwave. After the coating is melted add a few drops of green food coloring and stir. Add more if needed until the candy coating is a nice monster green.

3 Using a bamboo skewer, dip a large marshmallow into the candy coating until covered. Place on wax paper to allow to cool. Repeat until you have made 18 coated marshmallows.

4 Stir almond extract into the chocolate frosting. Then frost each cupcake.

5 Place one coated marshmallow in the center of each cupcake. Decorate with frosting and gels to create a mini Frankenstein head. Use a little extra frosting to stick green Mike and Ike candy "bolts" to the sides of the head. Finish off with more candies and sprinkles.

Swampy Dip

If you ever find yourself in a creepy swamp with hanging moss and weird noises, enjoy this tasty snack while you try to start the boat motor. Just make sure to keep your eyes on the water. You never know what may surface.

Makes 6 servings

1 (10-ounce) package frozen chopped spinach, thawed and drained

1 1/2 cups sour cream

3/4 cup mayonnaise

1 package vegetable dip mix

Vegetables to dip (mini carrots, cherry tomatoes, cucumber slices, broccoli florets)

Crackers to dip

1 Place all ingredients except vegetables and crackers in a medium-sized bowl. Mix well.

2 Chill in the refrigerator for 4 hours before serving. Serve with assorted fresh vegetables, crackers, and whatever other swamp flotsam you wish.

Monster-in-the-Moat Fondue

Legend has it that a certain castle in Switzerland was protected by a very ugly monster that lived in the surrounding moat. Make this moat fondue for all your monster friends.

Makes 4 to 6 servings

1 cup whipping cream

¼ cup chocolate drink mix (Nesquik)

1 tablespoon peanut butter

Fruit to dip (banana chunks, apple slices, strawberries)

Pretzels to dip

1 Using a whisk or electric mixer, beat together the whipping cream, chocolate drink mix, and peanut butter until smooth and the cream begins to thicken.

2 Pour into a serving bowl. Dip fruit pieces using bamboo skewers and pretzels by hand.

Swamp Gumbo

Down in the bayou, in the deepest, swampiest, most–monster infested part, this hearty gumbo warms up the most cowardly of hearts. Serve it with a nice chunk of French bread.

Makes 8 servings

1 pound ground turkey

1 small onion, chopped

1/2 teaspoon black pepper

1/2 teaspoon salt

1 teaspoon garlic powder

1/4 cup butter or margarine

1/3 cup flour

3 cups hot water

2 beef bouillon cubes

1 green bell pepper, seeded and chopped

3 stalks celery, chopped

1 tablespoon dried parsley

2 tablespoons Worcestershire sauce

1 (14.5-ounce) can diced tomatoes, with liquid

4 cups cooked white rice

1 In a skillet over medium-high heat, cook the ground turkey, breaking it apart. Add the chopped onion, pepper, salt, and garlic powder; cook for about 10 minutes or until the turkey is no longer pink. Drain the fat and set the mixture aside.

2 In a large, heavy stockpot, melt the butter over medium-high heat. Sprinkle with the flour and whisk to form a paste. Slowly stir in the hot water and crushed bouillon cubes.

3 Add the chopped green pepper and celery along with the parsley and Worcestershire sauce. Bring the mixture to a boil.

4 Add the cooked ground turkey and canned tomatoes. Cover and simmer for 15 minutes.

5 Serve in a bowl over 1/2 cup cooked white rice.

Punch from the Black Lagoon

You may have heard of the Creature from the Black Lagoon, but you've probably never heard of the punch. It is a closely held secret due to its delicious properties.

Makes 16 servings

2 liters lemon-lime soda, chilled

32 ounces grape juice, chilled

2 limes, sliced

1 quart lime sherbet

Fresh mint

1 In a large punch bowl mix the lemon-lime soda and the grape juice. Add half of the lime slices to the punch.

2 Remove the lime sherbet from the freezer and allow to soften slightly. Cover the surface of the punch with scoops of sherbet. Garnish with more limes and mint. Serve immediately.

Eyes-for-You Cupcakes

Here's looking at you, monster! This is a great treat to welcome new monster move-ins to the swamp!

Makes 24 cupcakes

1 box funfetti cake mix

1 can purchased
  vanilla frosting

Neon food coloring
  (blue, green, purple)

1 box white powdered
  mini donuts

Red decorating gel

1 package gumdrops or
  gummy Lifesaver candies

Brown mini M&Ms

Multicolored licorice twists

1 Prepare cupcakes according to directions on cake mix. Bake and allow to cool.

2 Divide the frosting into three small bowls. Add a few drops of food coloring to each and mix well. Frost the cupcakes using the different frostings.

3 On each mini donut, draw lines with the decorating gel to look like a bloodshot eye.

4 In the center of each donut place a gumdrop or gummy candy, securing it with a little bit of decorating gel. Add a brown mini M&M for the pupil.

5 Place one donut eye in the center of each cupcake. Use the licorice to create monster tentacles. Devour them before they devour you!

Coffin Critters Salad

A coffin really isn't that great of a resting place. A lot happens below ground. Slippery, slimy creatures of all sorts like to slide through your toes!

Makes 8 to 10 servings

1 (16-ounce) package spaghetti

1 cup wagon wheel pasta

1 roma tomato, chopped

1 cup cubed cheddar cheese

1 cucumber, peeled and chopped

1 cup green olives with pimento

1 (16-ounce) bottle low-fat Italian dressing

Salad seasoning

1 Following the package directions, boil the spaghetti, drain, and rinse with cold water. In a separate pan, boil the wagon wheel pasta, drain, and rinse with cold water. Place both pastas in a chilled serving bowl.

2 Add the tomato, cheese, cucumber, and olives. Pour in the Italian salad dressing and season to taste with salad seasoning.

3 Place the salad in the refrigerator overnight to marinate. This makes a delicious side dish to serve with Frankenfeet (page 40) or Wrap like a Mummy (page 30).

Misty Graveyard Chowder

Perfect for when you're chilled to the bone after a late night scavenging at the graveyard for "spare" parts. Enjoy this chowder with Garlicky Toast Stakes (page 22) for a pointed meal.

Makes 4 servings

1 tablespoon butter

1/2 cup chopped onion

1 1/2 cups water

2 cups chopped red
    potatoes, with skins

1 cup sliced carrots

1/4 teaspoon black pepper

1/2 teaspoon salt

1 (15-ounce) can kernel corn

1/2 cup diced ham (optional)

1 cup cream, chilled

1 tablespoon flour

1 cup grated cheddar cheese

1/2 cup sour cream

1 In a medium saucepan over medium heat, add the butter and onions. Cook, stirring frequently, until the onions are soft but not brown. Add water, potatoes, carrots, pepper, and salt.

2 Cover and simmer for about 15 minutes or until potatoes are tender.

3 Drain the can of corn. Add corn and ham, if using, to the chowder.

4 In a separate bowl, mix the flour into the cream and then slowly pour the mixture into the chowder while stirring. Continue to simmer, stirring frequently. When the chowder is thickened and bubbly, it is ready to serve.

5 Ladle chowder into bowls and garnish with grated cheese and a dollop of sour cream.

Sauces of the Undead with Nuggets

Zombies like their food really saucy. What is better than one sauce? How about three kinds, all sure to please even the pickiest denizens of darkness?

Serves 6 to 8 servings

2 pounds frozen popcorn chicken or nuggets

I cup mayonnaise, divided

2 tablespoons mustard

2 tablespoons honey

2 tablespoons chopped toasted pecans (optional)

I small can crushed pineapple

¾ cup barbecue sauce

¾ cup buttermilk

I tablespoon dried parsley

½ teaspoon black pepper

½ teaspoon onion powder

1 Follow the instructions on the package and bake the popcorn chicken or nuggets.

2 While the chicken is baking, prepare the three Sauces of the Undead.

3 Serve sauces and a large plate of chicken and get out of the way!

Monster Sting Sauce

Mix together ½ cup mayonnaise, ¼ cup mustard, and ¼ cup honey and blend well. Place in a small serving bowl and sprinkle with chopped toasted pecans if desired.

Howl-at-the-Moon Sauce

Open and drain the can of crushed pineapple. Mix with barbecue sauce. Place in a small serving bowl.

Palefaced Buttermilk Sauce

Combine ½ cup mayonnaise, buttermilk, parsley, pepper, and onion powder. Mix well and chill for at least 30 minutes. Place in a small serving bowl.

63

Zuppa di Zombie

In Italy, recently risen zombies like to kill time enjoying a sweet dessert known as Zuppa di Zombie. This recipe is also a great alternative for zombies on an all-brain diet.

Makes 6 servings

1 small package instant pistachio pudding

1 cup whipping cream

3 tablespoons powdered sugar

1/2 teaspoon vanilla extract

Blue food coloring

6 count package sponge cake rounds

Monster-themed breakfast cereal (such as Boo Berry or Count Chocula)*

Decorating sprinkles

*Other sweet breakfast cereal can be substituted.

1 Following the package directions, prepare the pistachio pudding and refrigerate. In a chilled bowl combine the whipping cream, powdered sugar, and vanilla. Beat with a wire whisk or electric mixer until peaks begin to form. Add a drop or two of blue food coloring.

2 Place one cake round in a small glass dish. Spoon about 1/3 cup of pudding onto the cake. Sprinkle the edges with monster cereal. Top with a dollop of whipped cream and sprinkles. Repeat for remaining cakes.